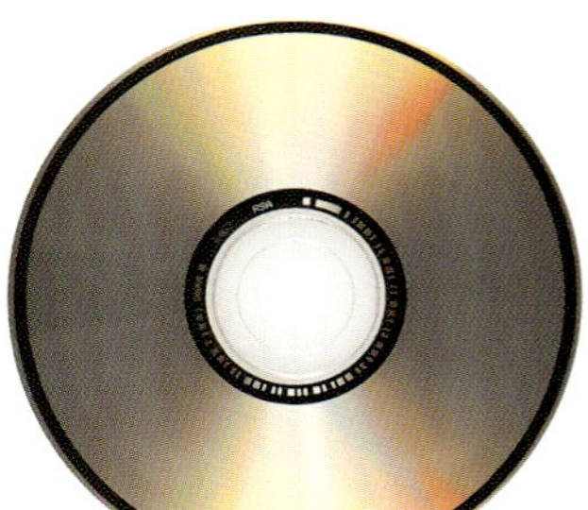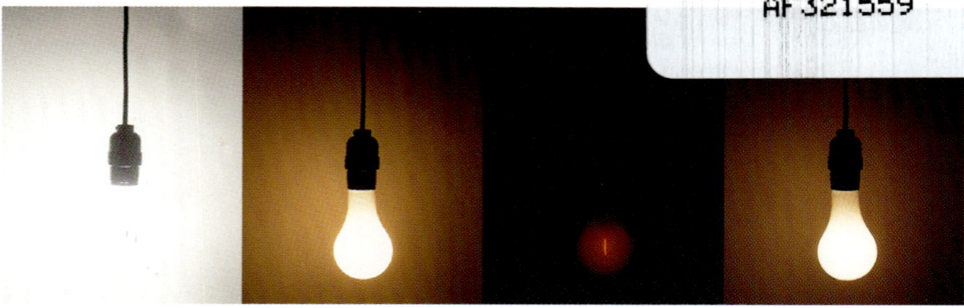

Force of dramatic character is transformed into pure energy. The light source, correlated to a sound organ, waxes and wanes according to the fluctuating intensity of the performed text.

Körperloses Aufflackern eines Bewusstseinsfunkens in der virtuellen Welt der Elektronik. Ein Son-et-lumière zur ephemeren Befindlichkeit des heutigen Menschen.

PARKETT 47

TONY OURSLER

TALKING LIGHT, 1996
CD of original script written and performed by the artist (running time approx. 15 minutes), standard 40 watt light bulb, sound organ kit (the light bulb reacts to the frequency of the voice on the CD); installation manual.
Ed. 50/XX, approx. **US$ 850**

TALKING LIGHT, 1996
CD mit der Stimme des Künstlers (Dauer ca. 15 Minuten), 40-Watt-Glühbirne, Tonverstärker mit Zubehör (die Glühbirne reagiert auf die Frequenzen der Stimme auf CD); Installationsanleitung.
Ed. 50/XX, ca. **sFr. 1000.–**

Riding the waves. A swell of words and images. Whooping with joy, seeking to maintain a precarious balance, persevering in focused silence.

Eine Welle von Worten und Bildern. Aufjauchzen, ums Gleichgewicht bangen, Labiles aushalten, still werden – kurz: Wellenreiten.

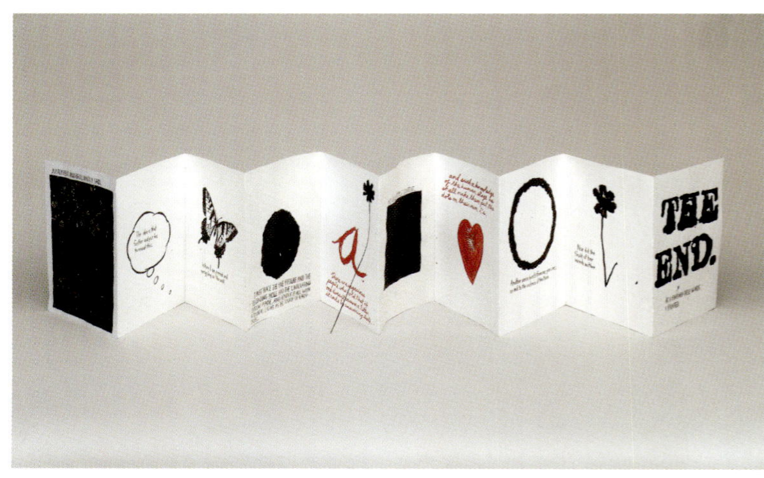

PARKETT 47

RAYMOND PETTIBON

UNTITLED (JUSTLY FELT AND BRILLIANTLY SAID), 1996
Silkscreen, hand-written texts by the artist which vary in each edition, pressed flower, printed by Lorenz Boegli, Zurich, on Arches 120 g, approx. $9\frac{5}{8}$ x $7\frac{5}{8}$", a 10-part foldout, full length $9\frac{5}{8}$ x $76\frac{3}{4}$".
Edition: 60/XX, signed and numbered, **US$ 750**

OHNE TITEL (JUSTLY FELT AND BRILLIANTLY SAID / RICHTIG EMPFUNDEN UND BRILLANT FORMULIERT), 1996
Siebdruck, mit handgeschriebenen Texten des Künstlers, die von Edition zu Edition variieren, gepresste Blume, gedruckt bei Lorenz Boegli, Zürich, auf Arches 120 g, ca. 24,5 x 195 cm (als 10teiliges Leporello gefalzt auf 24,5 x 19,5 cm).
Auflage: 60/XX, signiert und numeriert, **sFr. 850.–**

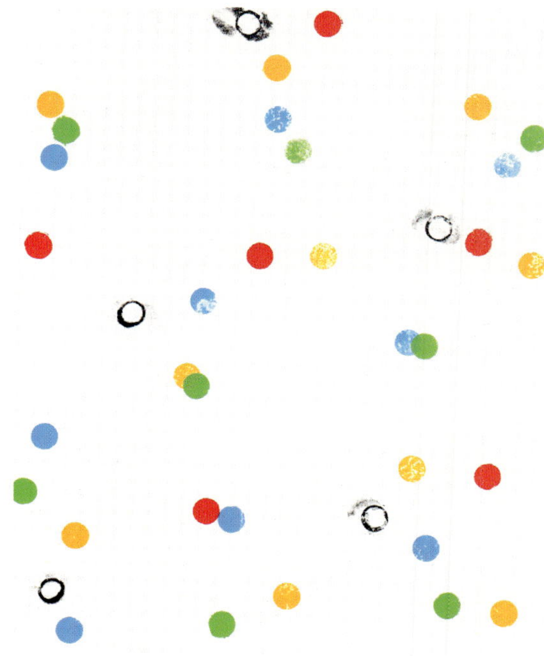

PARKETT 47

THOMAS SCHÜTTE
OLGA'S WALLPAPER, 1996 (1977)
Lithographie vom Stein, 5-farbig, gedruckt von Felix Bauer, Köln,
auf Indisches Handbütten, 250 g, ca. 102 x 68,5 cm
Ed. 60/XX, signiert und numeriert, **sFr. 850.–**

OLGA'S WALLPAPER, 1996 (1977)
Lithograph, stone-pulled, 5 colors, printed by Felix Bauer, Cologne,
on handmade Indian Vellum, 250 g, approx. $40\frac{1}{8}$ x 27"
Ed. 60/XX, signed and numbered, **US$ 750**

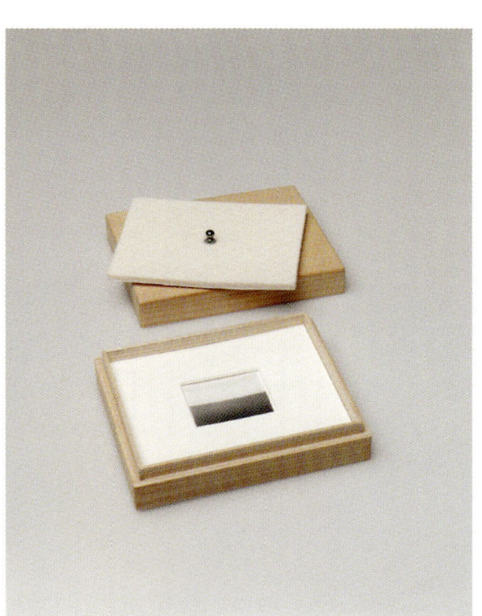
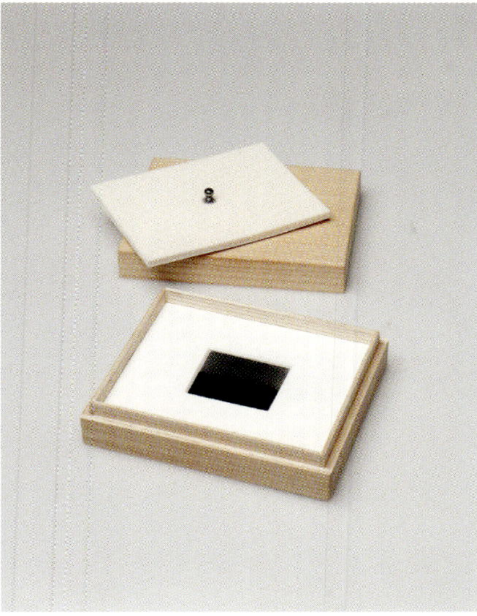

PARKETT 46

HIROSHI SUGIMOTO
**NIGHT SEASCAPE, IONIAN SEA,
SANTA CESAREA, 1990
DAY SEASCAPE, ENGLISH CHANNEL,
WESTON CLIFF, 1994**
miniature photography, paulownia box, rice paper
lined inner felt lid, silver plated knob (hand made in Japan)
image: 5,2 x 4,0 cm (approx. 2 x $1\frac{5}{8}$")
box: 15,8 x 12,8 x 4,6 cm (approx. $6\frac{1}{4}$ x 5 x $1\frac{3}{4}$")
Ed. of 35 each, signed and numbered, **US$ 950** each

**MEERESANSICHT BEI NACHT,
IONISCHES MEER, SANTA CESAREA, 1990
MEERESANSICHT BEI TAG, ÄRMELKANAL,
WESTON CLIFF, 1994**
Miniaturphotographie, Pauwlonia-Holzschachtel, Schutzfilz
mit Reispapierbelag und Silbergriff (japanische Handarbeit)
Bild: 5,2 x 4,0 cm
Schachtel: 15,8 x 12,8 x 4,6 cm
Ed. je 35, signiert und numeriert, je **sFr. 1140.–**

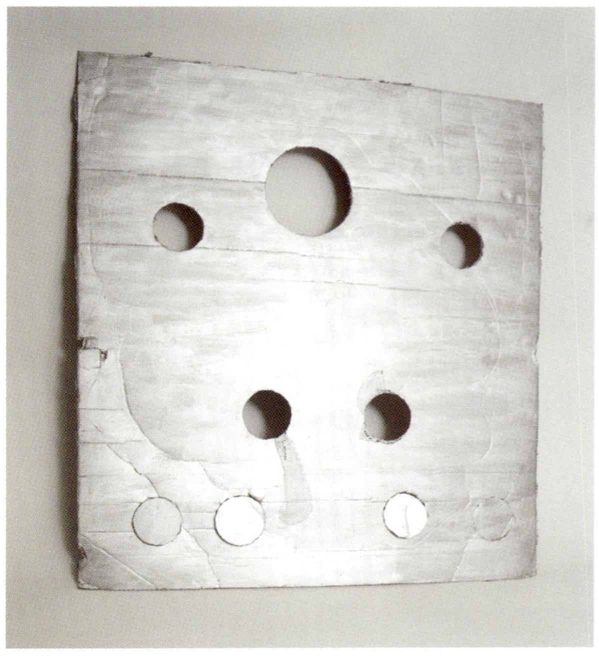

PARKETT 46

CADY NOLAND
(NOT YET TITLED), 1996
cardboard, lacquer-based sanding sealer and aluminum enamel spray paint
(please note: surface inflections differ from one piece to another) 56 x 54"
Ed. 50, signed and numbered, **US$ 850**

(NOCH OHNE TITEL), 1996
Pappkarton, Lackgrund und Aluminium-Farbspray (Bitte beachten: Falt-
und Biegespuren sind von Stück zu Stück verschieden), ca. 142 x 137 cm
Ed. 50, **sFr. 950.–**

PARKETT 45

SARAH LUCAS
LION HEART, 1995
cast metal, 50 pieces of cast lead, 50 pieces of
cast brass, produced at the Jäger Brothers Foundry,
Pfäffikon SZ, Switzerland,
approx. 2¾ x 2¾ x 1¾" each.
Ed. 100: No 1–50 (brass), No 51–100 (lead),
signed and numbered, **US$ 650**

LÖWENHERZ, 1995
Metallguss, 50 Exemplare in Bleilegierung,
50 Exemplare in Messing, gegossen durch
die Kunstgiesserei Gebrüder Jäger,
Pfäffikon SZ, Schweiz, je ca. 7 x 7 x 4,5 cm
Ed. 100: Nr. 1–50 (Messing), Nr. 51–100 (Blei),
signiert und numeriert, **sFr. 750.–**

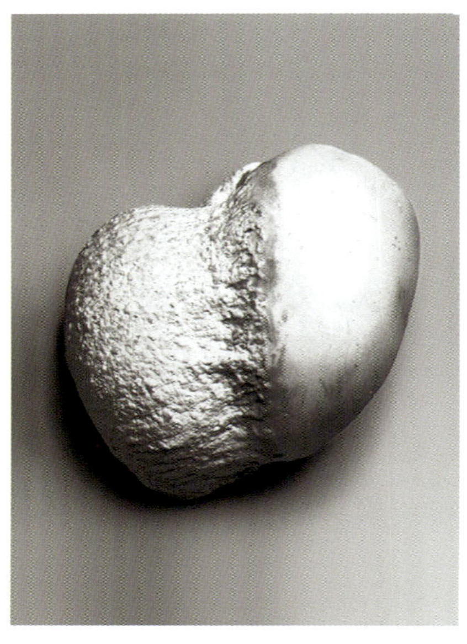
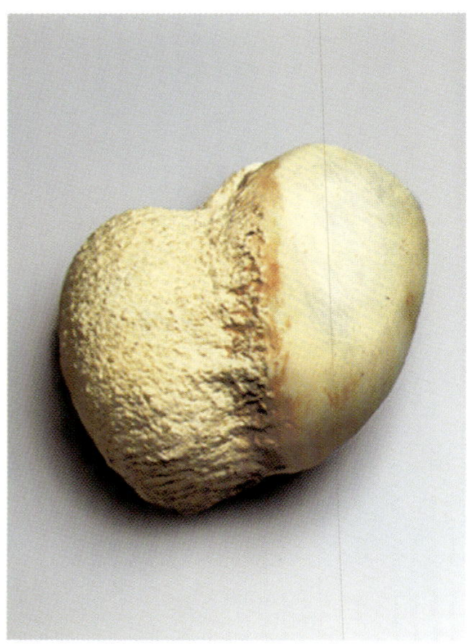

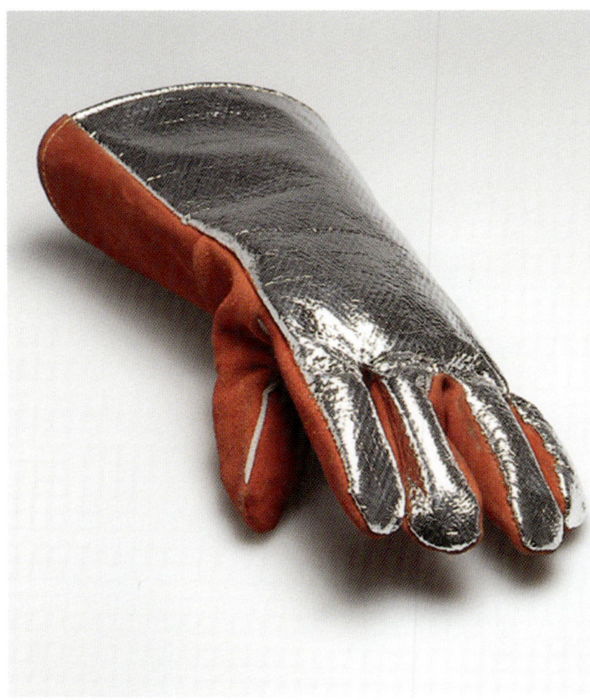

PARKETT 44

RIRKRIT TIRAVANIJA

UNTITLED, 1995 (450/375)
Gold-rimmed Ray Ban glasses with engraving on the lenses:
LONG RIVER   A SINGLE LINE
ORANGE SAFFRON   AT TWILIGHT
Ed. 80, numbered, with signed certificate, **US$ 780**

OHNE TITEL, 1995 (450/375)
Metallbrille Ray Ban mit Gravur auf den Gläsern:
LONG RIVER   A SINGLE LINE
ORANGE SAFFRON   AT TWILIGHT
Ed. 80, numeriert, mit signiertem Zertifikat, **sFr. 900.–**

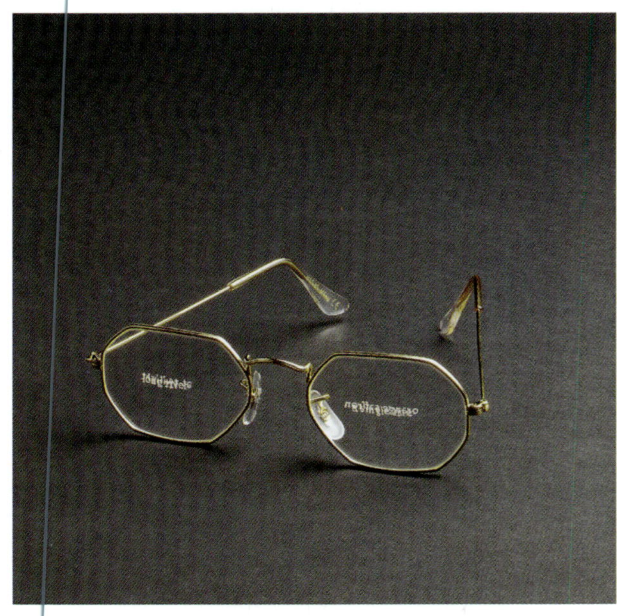

PARKETT 45

ROMAN SIGNER

FEUERWEHRHANDSCHUH MIT PHOTO, 1995
Handfläche aus hitzebeständigem Spezialspaltleder, Handrücken
aus hitzereflektierendem, aluminisiertem KEVLAR-Gewebe 550 g/m^2,
isolierendes Wollfutter, Länge 35 cm,
Photographie aus einem Video von Aleksandra Signer, ca. 13 x 18 cm
Ed. 80, signiert und numeriert, **sFr. 600.–**
FIREMAN'S GLOVE WITH PHOTOGRAPH, 1995
Standard fireman's glove with heat-resistant red suede palm, heat-reflecting,
aluminized KEVLAR back, 550 g/m^2, insulating woolen lining, length 13¾",
still from a video by Aleksandra Signer, approx. 5⅛ x 7⅛".
Ed. 80, signed and numbered, **US$ 520**

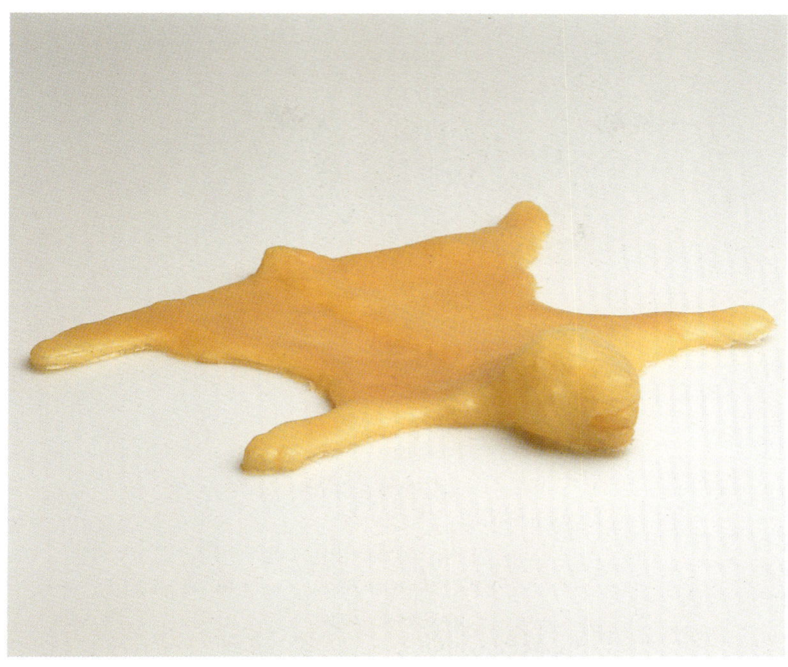

PARKETT 43

SUSAN ROTHENBERG
BEAR SKIN RUG 1995
Synthetic latex, $12\frac{1}{4}$ x $12\frac{1}{2}$ x 2"
Ed. 70, signed and numbered, **US$ 830**

BÄRENHAUT TEPPICH, 1995
Synthetischer Latex, 31 x 32 x 5 cm
Ed. 70, signiert und numeriert, **sFr. 950.–**

PARKETT 43

JUAN MUÑOZ
AUGENBLICK (GLIMPSE), 1995
Hand-etched glass. The image becomes
momentarily visible by breathing on the glass.
$4\frac{3}{4}$ x $3\frac{1}{2}$ x $\frac{1}{8}$"
Ed. 70, signed and numbered, **US$ 830**

AUGENBLICK, 1995
Hand-Radierung auf Glas. Das Bild wird sicht-
bar durch Anhauchen des Glases. 12 x 9 x 0,3 cm
Ed. 70, signiert und numeriert, **sFr. 950.–**

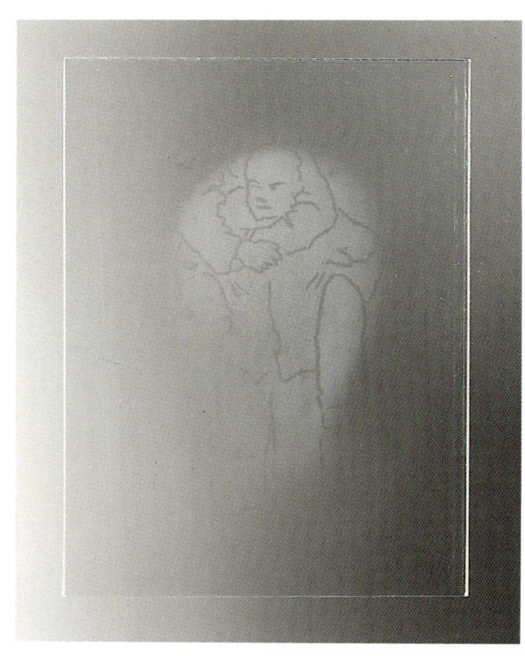

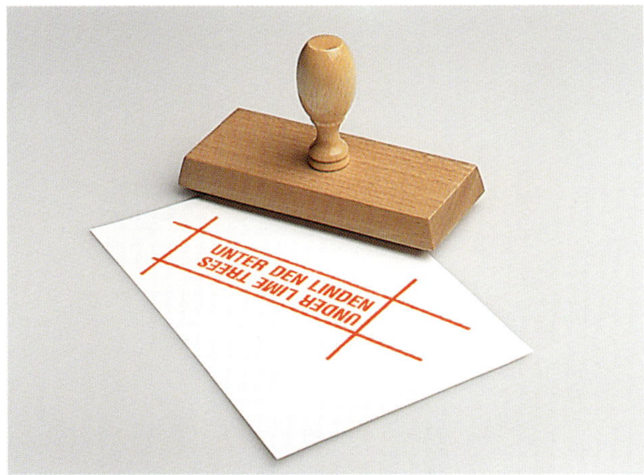

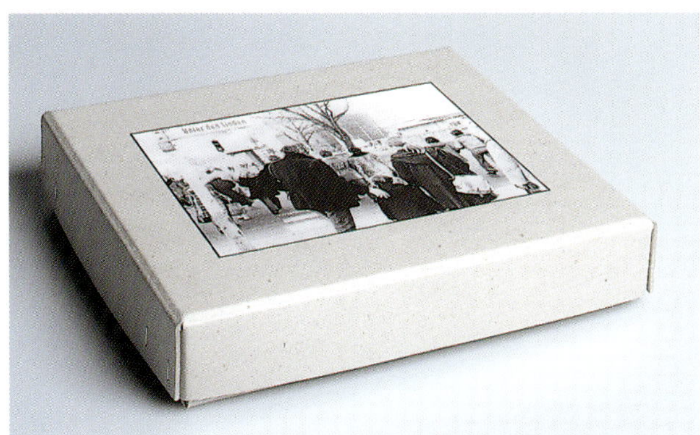

PARKETT 42

LAWRENCE WEINER

UNTER DEN LINDEN – UNDER LIME TREES, 1994
Stamp 7⅝ x 3¾ x 3½" with red ink pad
in silkscreened cardboard box.
Ed. 80, signed and numbered, US$ **740**

UNTER DEN LINDEN – UNDER LIME TREES, 1994
Stempel 19,5 x 9,5 x 9 cm mit
rotem Stempelkissen in Kartonschachtel,
Feinrastersiebdruck.
Ed. 80, signiert und numeriert, **sFr. 850.–**

PARKETT 40/41

SIGMAR POLKE

OHNE TITEL, 1994
Parkett-Band aus Überdruck-Makulatur, 25,5 x 21 cm, Ed. 25,
signiert und numeriert, **sFr. 2000.–**

UNTITLED, 1994
Volume of Parkett made of overprint paper, 10 x 8¼", Ed. 25
copies, signed and numbered, **US$ 1740**

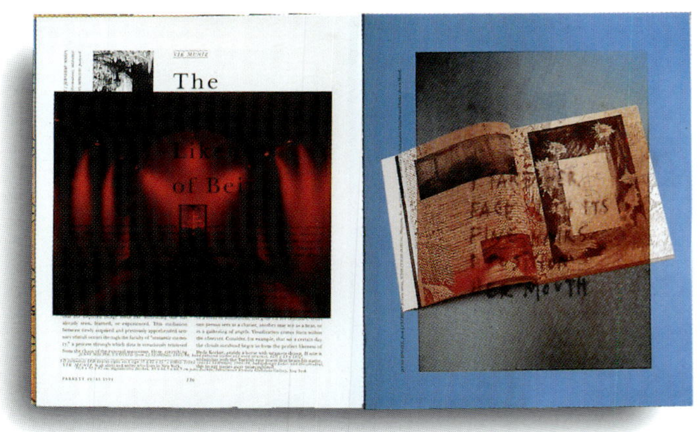

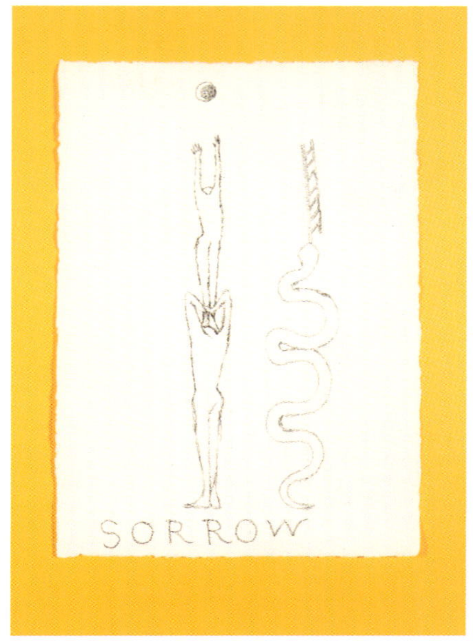

FRANCESCO CLEMENTE
SORROW, 1994
Tiefdruck mit Photoätzung, 29 x 20,5 cm,
gedruckt bei Peter Kneubühler, Zürich,
auf handgeschöpftem Bütten-Papier,
Ed. 60, signiert und numeriert, **sFr. 1500.–**
SORROW, 1994
Photo-etching, printed by Peter Kneubühler
on handmade Vellum, 11⅛ x 8⅛", Ed. 60,
signed and numbered, **US$ 1300**

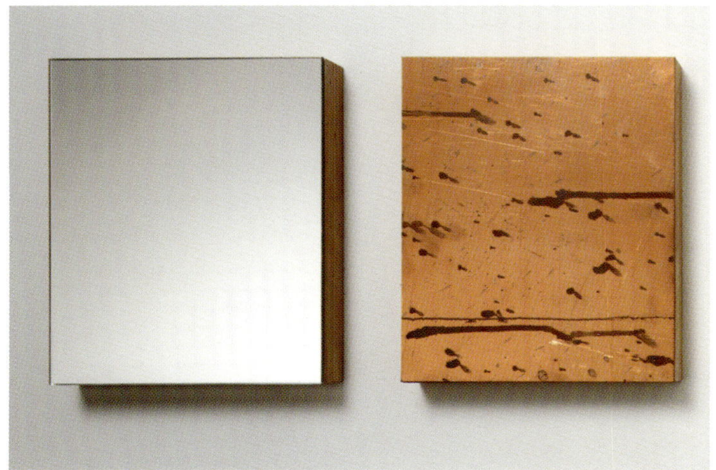

GÜNTHER FÖRG
OHNE TITEL (FÜR PARKETT), 1994
Zweiteiliges Objekt mit je einem Spiegel und
einer Kupferplatte, auf Holz montiert, im
Parkett-Format, je 25,5 x 21 x 3,2 cm,
Ausführung Jürgen Zimmermann, Karlsruhe,
Ed. 45, signiert und numeriert, **sFr. 2200.–**
UNTITLED (FOR PARKETT), 1994
Two-part object, consisting of one mirror and
one copperplate each mounted on wood in
Parkett format, each 10 x 8¼ x 1¼",
produced by Jürgen Zimmermann, Karlsruhe,
Ed. 45, signed and numbered, **US$ 1910**

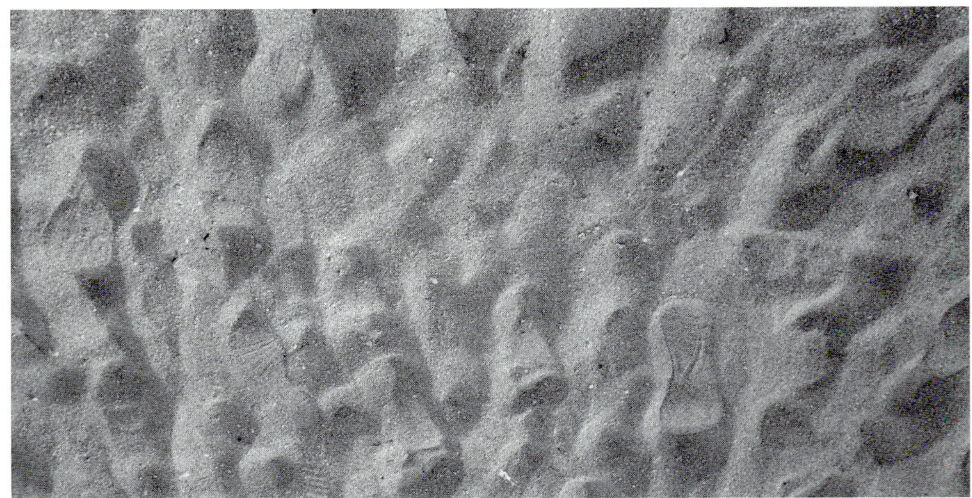

FELIX GONZALEZ-TORRES
OHNE TITEL (FÜR PARKETT), 1994
Plakat in 8 Blätter unterteilt, Siebdruck auf im-
prägniertem (Appleton-)Papier, 317,5 x 690,9 cm,
Ed. 84, signiert und numeriert, **sFr. 1500.–**
UNTITLED (FOR PARKETT), 1994
8-sheet billboard, silkscreen on Appleton
coated stock, 125 x 272",
Ed. 84, signed and numbered, **US$ 1300**

WOLFGANG LAIB
A WAX ROOM FOR A MOUNTAIN, 1994
Vom Künstler mit Ölstift überarbeiteter Siebdruck
auf Rivoli SK2 (240 g), gedruckt bei Lorenz
Boegli, Zürich, 49,3 x 41 cm,
Ed. 75, signiert und numeriert, **sFr. 900.–**
A WAX ROOM FOR A MOUNTAIN, 1994
Silkscreen, oilstick on Rivoli SK2 (240 g),
printed by Lorenz Boegli, Zurich, 19½ x 16⅛",
Ed. 75, signed and numbered, **US$ 780**

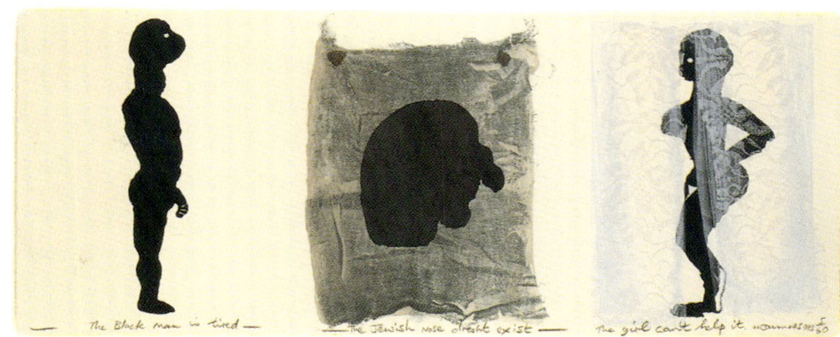

MARLENE DUMAS
THE BLACK MAN, THE JEW, AND THE GIRL, 1993
Triptych printed by Marcel Kalksma, Amsterdam, in three processes on 250 grs Arches: Blockprint in one color, two transfer lithographs from one stone rendered in two colors, inked and inscribed by hand, with eyes and organs scratched out, folded zigzag, 10 x 24¾",
Ed. 60, signed and numbered, **US$ 1040**
THE BLACK MAN, THE JEW, AND THE GIRL, 1993
Gefaltetes Triptychon, hergestellt bei Marcel Kalksma, Amsterdam, in drei Durchgängen auf Arches (250 g): einfarbiger Holzschnitt (Silhouetten), zweifache Umdrucklithographie von einem Stein in zwei Farben, mit Tinte markiert, Augen und Geschlechtsteile ausgekratzt, handschriftlicher Text, 25,5 x 63 cm, Ed. 60, signiert und numeriert, **sFr. 1200.–**

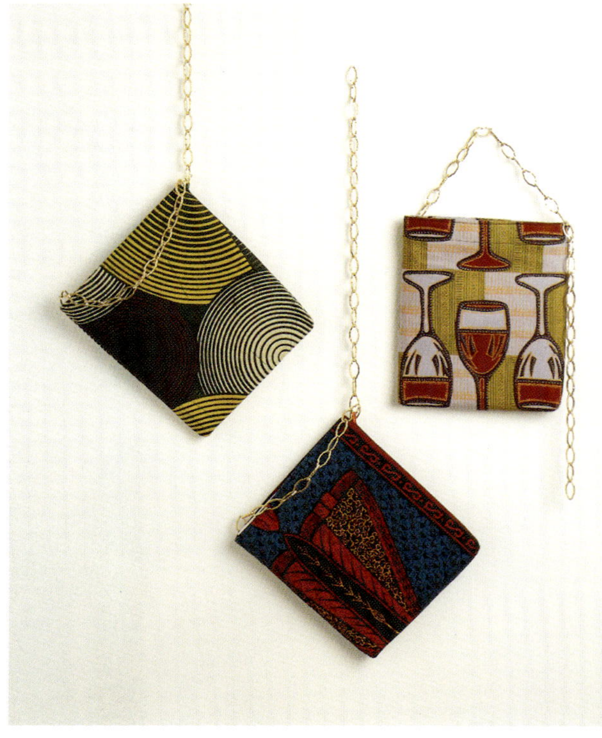

FRANZ WEST
ETUI FÜR PARKETT, 1993
Bedruckte afrikanische Baumwollstoffe, Kette,
Ed. 180, signiert und numeriert, **sFr. 300.–**
POUCH FOR PARKETT, 1993
Printed African fabric, chain, Ed. 180,
signed and numbered, **US$ 260**

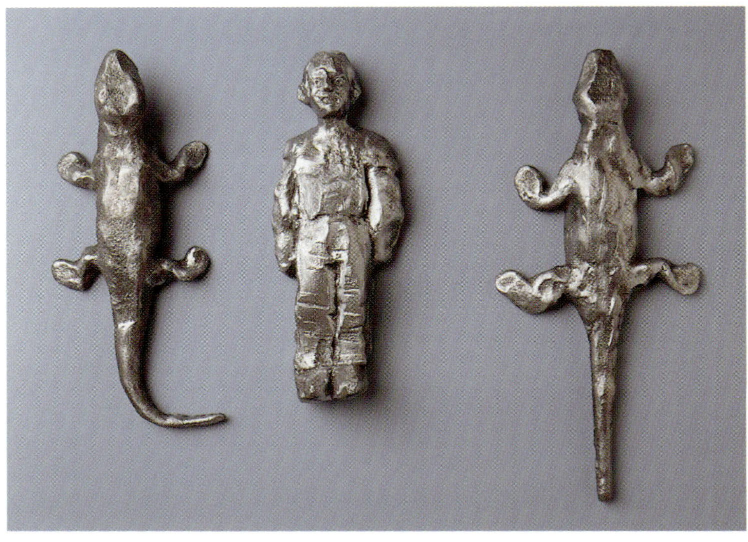

PARKETT 36

STEPHAN BALKENHOL
ZWEI ECHSEN MIT MANN, 1993
Dreiteilige Figurengruppe, gegossen in
Bleilegierung durch Giesserei Bärtschi, Aefligen,
Schweiz, je ca. 30 x 13 x 4 cm, Gewicht je ca. 2 kg,
Ed. 85, signiert und numeriert, **sFr. 1900.–**
TWO LIZARDS AND A MAN, 1993
Group of three cast lead figurines, produced
at the Bärtschi Foundry, Aefligen, Switzerland,
each figure approx. $11\frac{7}{8}$ x $5\frac{1}{8}$ x $1\frac{1}{2}$", weighing
approx. 4.5 lbs, Ed. 85, signed and
numbered, **US$ 1650**

PARKETT 36

SOPHIE CALLE
THE TIE, 1993
Krawatte mit aufgedruckter Kurzgeschichte
«I saw him», Crêpe de Chine,
braun mit blauem Text, hergestellt durch
Fabric Frontline, Zürich, Ed. 150,
signiert und numeriert, **sFr. 280.–**
THE TIE, 1993
Pure silk crepe-de-chine man's tie, printed
with an autobiographical story,
produced by Fabric Frontline, Zurich,
Ed. 150, signed and numbered, **US$ 243**

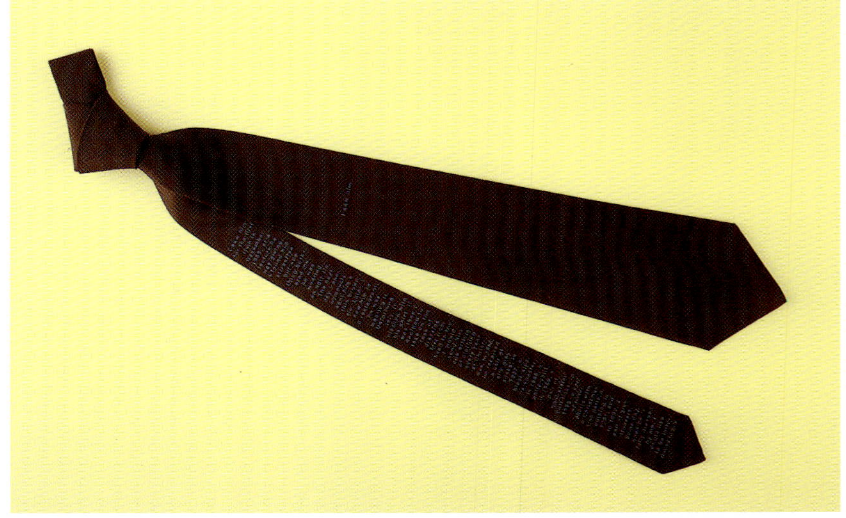

PARKETT 34

RICHARD PRINCE
GOOD REVOLUTION, 1992

Goldene Schallplatte und graviertes Metallschild auf C-Print, montiert und
gerahmt. Enthält zusätzlich eine beidseitig abspielbare Vinylplatte des Künstlers.
«Good Revolution» (1,46 Min.) und «Don't Belong» (1,46 Min.) arrangiert und
interpretiert von Richard Prince. Aufgenommen und gemischt auf der
Harmonic Ranch von Mark Degliantoni, September 1992. 52 x 41,9 cm.
Ed. 80, signiert und numeriert, **sFr. 1100.–**

GOOD REVOLUTION, 1992

Presentation gold record with engraved plaque mounted on C-Print, framed.
Includes a playable vinyl record by the artist, recorded on both sides.
"Good Revolution" (1:46) and "Don't Belong" (1:46), arranged and
performed by Richard Prince. Recorded and mixed at Harmonic Ranch
by Mark Degliantoni, September 1992. 20½ x 16½" (52 x 41,9 cm),
Ed. 80, signed and numbered, **US$ 960**

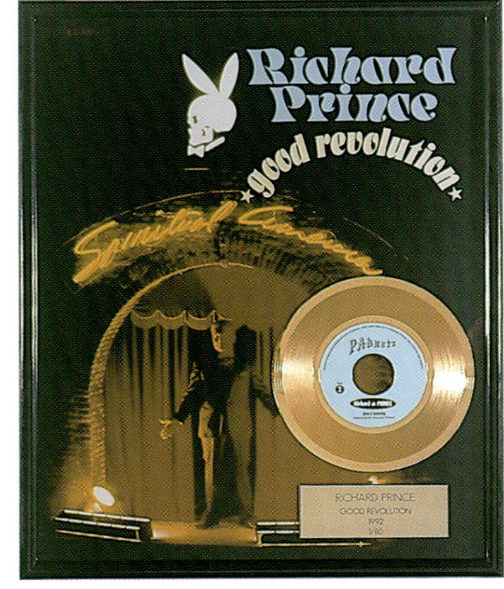

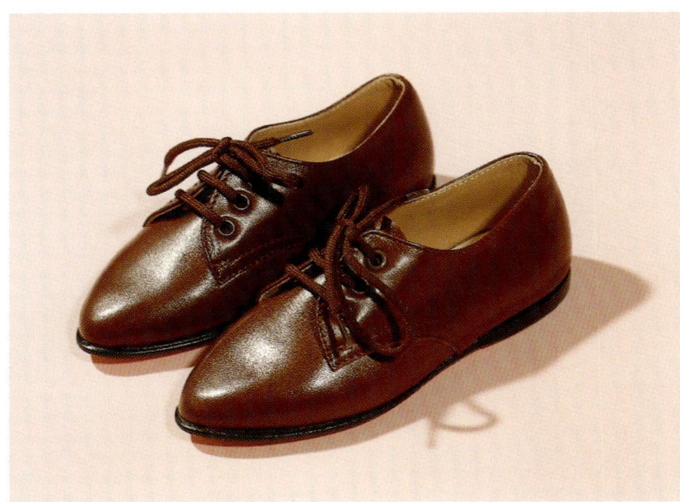

PARKETT 32

SHERRIE LEVINE
2 SCHUHE, 1992

Ein Paar Kinderschuhe, braunes Leder, je ca. 16 x 6 x 6 cm,
Ed. 99, signiert und numeriert, **sFr. 830.–**

2 SHOES, 1992

Pair of shoes, brown leather, each 6½ x 2½ x 2½"
(16 x 6 x 6 cm), Ed. 99, signed and numbered, **US$ 720**

FRANZ GERTSCH
CIMA DEL MAR (AUSSCHNITT), 1990/91
Holzschnitt (Kobalttürkis und Ultramarin, halb und halb) auf
Heizoburo-Japanpapier, 25,4 x 41,6 cm, gefaltet, nicht eingebunden,
Ed. 80, signiert und numeriert, **sFr. 1350.–**
CIMA DEL MAR (DETAIL), 1990/91
Woodcut (cobalt turquoise and ultramarine, half and half) on
Heizoburo Japan paper, 10 x 16⅜" (25,4 x 41,6 cm), folded, not bound
in the magazine, Ed. 80, signed and numbered, **US$ 1170**

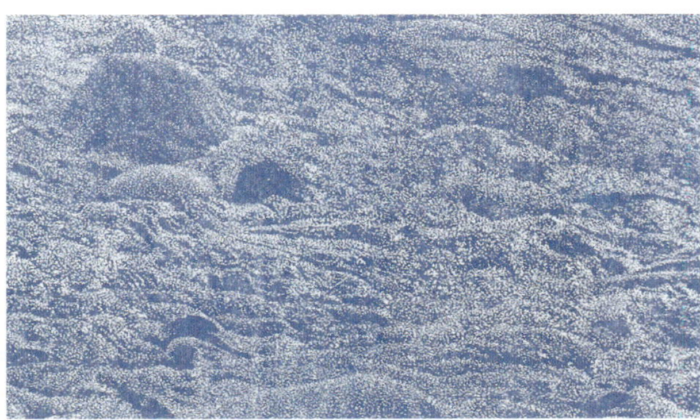

Detail aus einem über zwei Meter hohen Holzstock, an dem Franz
Gertsch ein Jahr lang gearbeitet hat.

Against the grain. Every point of light on this minutely described
surface corresponds to the removal of a sliver of wood. This fragment
was taken from a gigantic woodcut measuring more than 5 x 6 feet
(170 x 152 cm).

Ein Monster, gedruckt auf feinste Seide, quillt
aus einem Goldrahmen.

The little house of horrors. A silken greasepaint
grotesque rendered in startling 3-D threatens
to burst from its keepsake frame.

Basketball ist eine der Möglichkeiten für einen Afro-Amerikaner,
reich zu werden. So trägt die Photographie des Objet trouvé den
Titel «Geldbaum».

Readymade magic. A basketball hoop fashioned from the rim of a
bicycle tire, embedded in a living tree in a Charleston backyard,
testifies to the ingenuity of its anonymous maker.

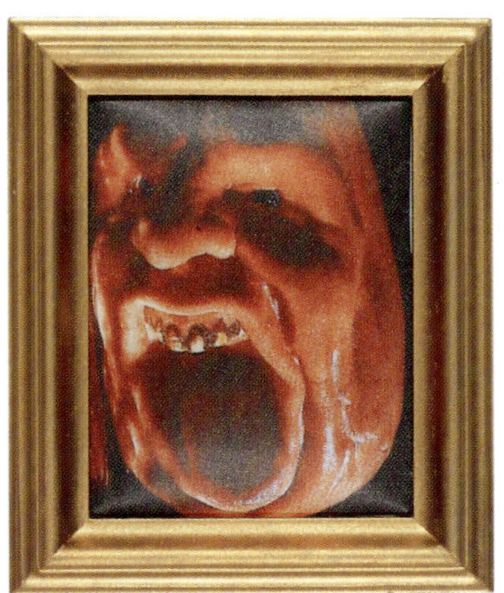

PARKETT 29

CINDY SHERMAN
OHNE TITEL, 1991
Bedruckte Seide, gepolstert, in goldfarbenem
Holzrahmen, 15 x 11,5 cm (Bild),
21,3 x 17,4 cm (Rahmen), Ed. 100, signiert
und numeriert, **sFr. 1380.–**
UNTITLED, 1991
Printed silk, padded, in gilded wooden
frame, 8⅜ x 6⅞" (21,3 x 17,4 cm), with frame,
Ed. 100, signed and numbered, **US$ 1200**

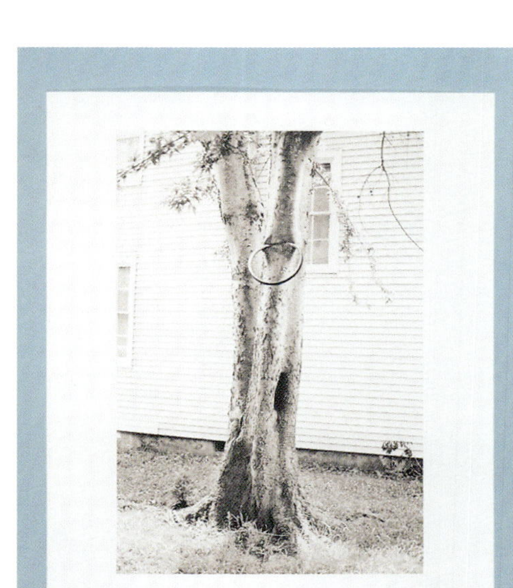

DAVID HAMMONS
GELDBAUM, 1992
Sepia-Print-Photographie,
42 x 28 cm, Ed. 70,
signiert und numeriert,
sFr. 890.–
MONEY TREE, 1992
Sepia-Print photograph,
16½ x 11" (42 x 28 cm),
Ed. 70, signed and
numbered, **US$ 770**

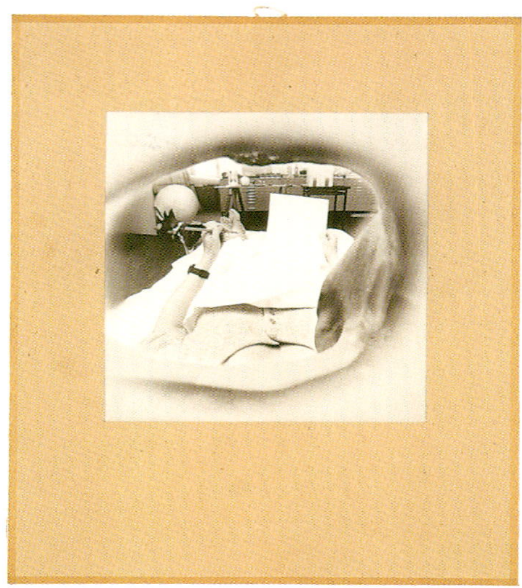

PARKETT 33

ROSEMARIE TROCKEL
STUDIO VISIT, 1992

Photogravure in Strohpappe-Passepartout mit Prägedruck, säurefreies Folienfenster, auf Holz montiert mit Aufhänger, Bild: 21 x 21 cm, Rahmen: 38 x 33 x 0,9 cm, Ed. 80, signiert und numeriert, **sFr. 850.–**

STUDIO VISIT, 1992

Photoetching and acid-free transparent foil in embossed strawboard matte, mounted on wood with hanger, image: 8¼ x 8¼", frame: 15 x 13 x ⅜", Ed. 80, signed and numbered, **US$ 740**

Printed by Peter Kneubühler

PARKETT 28

THOMAS RUFF
C-PRINTS, 1991

2 C-Prints (Photos: ESO), je 50 x 50 cm, in Transparenthüllen, astronomische Daten in Siebdruck beidseitig auf Hüllen gedruckt, Ed. je 50, signiert und numeriert, **sFr. 1200.–**

C-PRINTS, 1991

Two c-prints (Photos: ESO), each 19½ x 19½" (50 x 50 cm), with astronomic data silk-screened on front and back of transparent wrappers, Ed. of 50 each, signed and numbered, **US$ 1040**

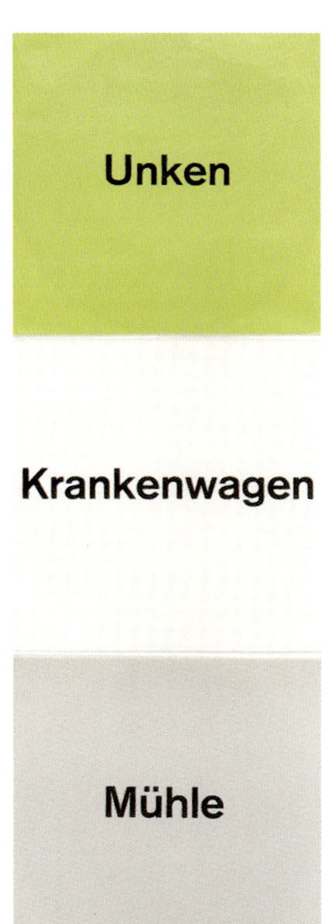

PARKETT 25

KATHARINA FRITSCH
MÜHLE / KRANKENWAGEN /
UNKEN, 1990
Drei Single-Schallplatten, Ed. je 2000,
unsigniert, zusammen: **sFr. 45.–**
MILL / AMBULANCE / TOADS,
1990
Set of three single records, Ed. of 2000
sets, unsigned, for set of three: **US$ 39**

Klang- und Geräuschskulpturen, Erinnerungsbilder aus dem kollektiven Gedächtnis formen sich aus Ihren Lautsprechern heraus.

Music for the eyes. A set of three records, each pressed with a single ambient sound from the artist's aural memory—toads croaking, a watermill churning, a local ambulance siren wailing—and sealed with a corresponding emblematic color.

Licht materialisiert sich zu geometrischen Körpern; für einmal nicht in einer von Turrells Rauminstallationen, sondern in einem traditionsgemäss für Hell-Dunkel-Effekte geschaffenen Medium.

Speed of light. These experimental forays into the medium of etching yield light as material, not illusion, in the contours of the printed image.

PARKETT 25

JAMES TURRELL
SQUAT, CARN, 1990
Aquatinta-Editionen auf Zerkall 250 g, je 25,5 x 21 cm, in Parkett
eingebunden, Ed. je 40 pro Aquatinta,
signiert und numeriert, **sFr. 1200.–** pro Aquatinta
SQUAT, CARN, 1990
Aquatint editions on Zerkall 250 g, each 10 x 8¼"
(25,5 x 21 cm), bound in the magazine. Ed. of 40 each, signed
and numbered, **US$ 1040** per print

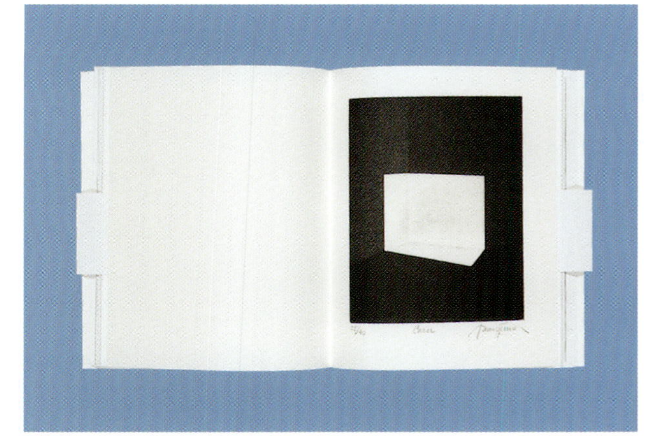

ALEX KATZ
SCHWARZER TEICH, 1989
Holzschnitt auf Goyu-Papier, 29,5 x 46 cm,
Ed. 100, signiert und numeriert, **sFr. 950.–**
BLACK POND, 1989
Woodcut on Goyu paper,
11⅝ x 18⅛" (29,5 x 46 cm),
Ed. 100, signed and numbered, **US$ 830**

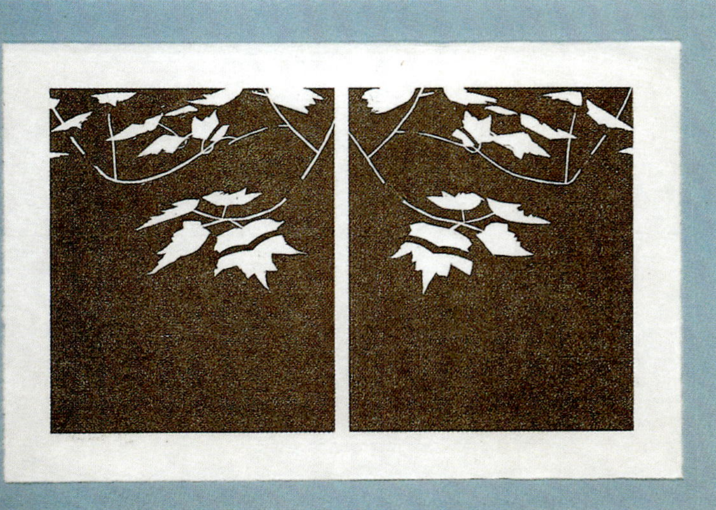

ALIGHIERO E BOETTI
AUF DEN SPUREN DER GEHEIMNISSE
EINES DOPPELLEBENS, 1990
Lichtdruck (Granolitho), von Hand rot übermalt,
50 x 70 cm, Ed. 100, signiert und numeriert, **sFr. 1200.–**
PROBING THE MYSTERIES
OF A DOUBLE LIFE, 1990
Collotype (Granolitho), overpainted by
hand in red, 19⅝ x 27½" (50 x 70 cm),
Ed. 100, signed and numbered, **US$ 1040**

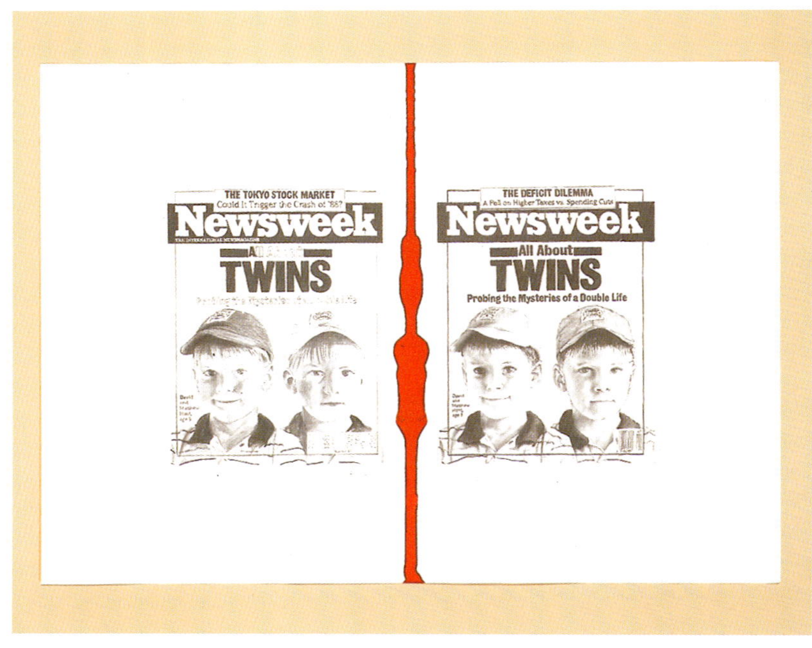

PARKETT 16

ROBERT WILSON
A LETTER FOR QUEEN VICTORIA, 1988
Lithographie auf Rives, 25,5 x 61 cm, in Parkett eingebunden,
Ed. 80, signiert und numeriert, **sFr. 800.–**
Lithograph on Rives, 10 x 24", (25,5 x 61 cm), bound in the magazine,
Ed. 80, signed and numbered, **US$ 690**
Printed by Champfleury

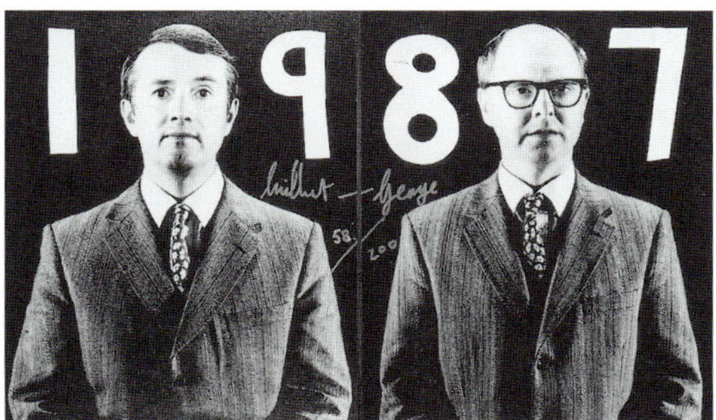

PARKETT 14

GILBERT & GEORGE, 1987
Photographie auf Karton aufgezogen,
in der Mitte faltbar, 25,5 x 42 cm,
Ed. 200, signiert und numeriert, **sFr. 1200.–**
Photograph, mounted on cardboard
folded in the middle, 10 x 16½" (25,5 x 42 cm),
Ed. 200, signed and numbered, **US$ 1040**

The PARKETT Series is created in collaboration with artists, who contribute an original work available exclusively to the subscribers in the form of a signed limited SPECIAL EDITION. The available works are also reproduced in each PARKETT issue.

Each SPECIAL EDITION is available by order from any one of our offices in New York or Zurich. Just fill in the details below and send this card to the office nearest you. Once your order has been processed, you will be issued with an invoice and your personal edition number. Upon receipt of payment, you will receive the SPECIAL EDITION. (Please note that supply is subject to availability. PARKETT does not assume responsibility for any delays in production of SPECIAL EDITIONS. Postage is not included.)

◼ As a subscriber to PARKETT, I would like to order the following Special Edition(s), signed and numbered by the artist.

PARKETT No.	ARTIST	NAME:
PARKETT No.	ARTIST	ADDRESS:
PARKETT No.	ARTIST	CITY:
PARKETT No.	ARTIST	STATE/ZIP:
PARKETT No.	ARTIST	COUNTRY:
PARKETT No.	ARTIST	PHONE:

◼ I have indicated my way of payment on the reverse side of this form.

Send this form to the PARKETT office nearest you:

PARKETT PUBLISHERS   155 AV. OF THE AMERICAS   NEW YORK, NY 10013   PHONE (212) 673-2660   FAX (212) 271-0704

PARKETT VERLAG   QUELLENSTRASSE 27   CH-8005 ZÜRICH   TELEFON +41-1-271 81 40   FAX +41-1-272 43 01

PARKETT VERLAG   TANNENWALDALLEE 17   D-61348 BAD HOMBURG   FAX 06172-937 444

PÄRKETT

KÜNSTLEREDITIONEN FÜR PARKETT-ABONNENTEN

47

Die PARKETT-Buchreihe entsteht in Zusammenarbeit mit Künstlern, die eigens für die Abonnenten einen Originalbeitrag in Form einer limitierten und signierten EDITION gestalten. Diese Editionen sind auch in der Zeitschrift abgebildet und können mit dieser Bestellkarte in jedem unserer Büros in Zürich, Frankfurt oder New York bestellt werden. Sie erhalten dann Ihre persönliche Editionsnummer und eine Rechnung. Sobald wir Ihre Zahlung erhalten haben, schicken wir Ihnen Ihre Edition(en). (Lieferung nur solange vorrätig. PARKETT übernimmt keine Verantwortung für allfällige Verzögerungen bei der Herstellung der Vorzugsausgaben. Versandkosten zuzüglich.)

◼ Ich bin PARKETT-Abonnent(in) und bestelle folgende EDITION(EN), numeriert und vom Künstler signiert:

PARKETT Nr.	KÜNSTLER/IN	NAME:
PARKETT Nr.	KÜNSTLER/IN	STRASSE:
PARKETT Nr.	KÜNSTLER/IN	PLZ/STADT:
PARKETT Nr.	KÜNSTLER/IN	LAND:
PARKETT Nr.	KÜNSTLER/IN	TEL.:

◼ Meine Zahlungsweise habe ich auf der Rückseite angegeben.

Schicken Sie diese Bestellkarte an das PARKETT-Büro in Ihrer Nähe:

PARKETT VERLAG   QUELLENSTRASSE 27   CH-8005 ZÜRICH   TELEFON +41-1-271 81 40   FAX +41-1-272 43 01

PARKETT VERLAG   TANNENWALDALLEE 17   D-61348 BAD HOMBURG   FAX 06172-937 444

PARKETT PUBLISHERS   155 AV. OF THE AMERICAS   NEW YORK, NY 10013   PHONE (212) 673-2660   FAX (212) 271-0704

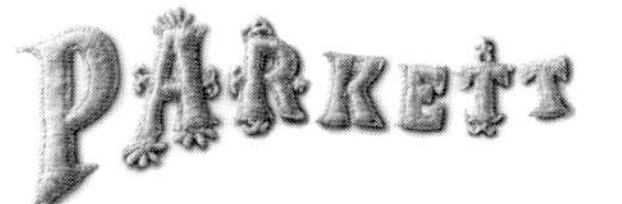

SUBSCRIBE, COMPLETE OR SEND A GIFT SUBSCRIPTION TO THE BEST BOOK SERIES ON CONTEMPORARY ARTISTS

- ☐ I subscribe to the PARKETT series
  - ☐ for 1 year (3 issues) at US$ 75 (USA/Canada), SFr. 115.– (Europe), SFr. 130.– (Rest of the world; by air mail: SFr. 210.–)
  - ☐ for 2 years (6 issues) at US$ 135 (USA/Canada), SFr. 205.– (Europe), SFr. 240.– (Rest of the world; air mail: SFr. 395.–)
  - ☐ for 1 year (3 issues) at a 20% student discount (US$ 60 for USA/Canada, SFr. 91.– for Europe). A copy of my student ID is enclosed.

- ☐ Send a gift subscription in my name
  - ☐ for 1 year (3 issues) at US$ 75 (USA/Canada), SFr. 115.– (Europe), SFr. 130.– (Rest of the world; by air mail: SFr. 210.–)
  - ☐ for 2 years (6 issues) at US$ 135 (USA/Canada), SFr. 205.– (Europe), SFr. 240.– (Rest of the world; air mail: SFr. 395.–)
  - A gift card in my name will be sent to the recipient.

Postage included. All prices subject to change.

- ☐ I wish to complete my PARKETT collection and order the following issue no(s):
  ____
  at SFr. 39.– each (up to no. 43: SFr. 30.–), postage not included. Within the USA & Canada $ 29.00 (up to no. 43: $ 19.50), add postage: $ 5 (USA), $ 10 (Canada). (Sold out: No. 1–10, 27, 29–31, 35)

- ☐ I wish to order the catalog raisonné of all PARKETT Artists' Editions from 1984–95 (SILENT & VIOLENT, 183 pages of which 144 in color, text by Susan Tallman, short artists' biographies) for Sfr. 49.– (USA: $ 39.00), excl. postage.

- ☐ I wish to order _________ copies of the set of 36 postcards featuring PARKETT Artists' Editions for Sfr. 19.– (USA: $ 16.00) per set, excl. postage.

NAME: ________________________________

ADDRESS: ________________________________

CITY: ________________________________

STATE/ZIP: ________________________________

COUNTRY: ________________________________

TEL.: _____________________ FAX: _____________________

GIFT RECIPIENT: ________________________________

ADDRESS: ________________________________

CITY: ________________________________

STATE/ZIP : ________________________________

COUNTRY: ________________________________

☐ Charge my Visa Card ☐ Mastercard ☐ AMEX

Card No. [| | | | | | | | | | | | | |] Expiration date _________

☐ Payment enclosed (US check or money order)

DATE _______________________________

SIGNATURE _______________________________

Send this form to the PARKETT office nearest you:

PARKETT PUBLISHERS 155 AV. OF THE AMERICAS NEW YORK, NY 10013 PHONE (212) 673-2660 FAX (212) 271-0704

PARKETT VERLAG QUELLENSTRASSE 27 CH-8005 ZÜRICH TELEFON +41-1-271 81 40 FAX +41-1-272 43 01

PARKETT VERLAG TANNENWALDALLEE 17 D-61348 BAD HOMBURG FAX 06172-937 444

ABONNIEREN, VERVOLLSTÄNDIGEN ODER VERSCHENKEN SIE DIE UMFASSENDSTE BUCHREIHE ÜBER GEGENWARTSKÜNSTLER

- ☐ Ich abonniere die PARKETT-Reihe
  - ☐ für 1 Jahr (3 Ausgaben) zu:
    DM 122,– (BRD), SFr. 98.– (Schweiz), SFr. 115.– (übriges Europa).
  - ☐ für 2 Jahre (6 Ausgaben) zu:
    DM 222,– (BRD), SFr. 176.– (Schweiz), SFr. 205.– (übriges Europa).
  - ☐ für 1 Jahr (3 Ausgaben) mit 20% Studentenermässigung
    (BRD: DM 97,–/Schweiz: SFr. 78.–/Europa: SFr. 91.–).
    Eine Kopie meines Studentenausweises lege ich bei.

- ☐ Ich verschenke ein PARKETT-Abonnement
  - ☐ für 1 Jahr (3 Ausgaben) zu:
    DM 122,– (BRD), SFr. 98.– (Schweiz), SFr. 115.– (übriges Europa).
  - ☐ für 2 Jahre (6 Ausgaben) zu:
    DM 222,– (BRD), SFr. 176.– (Schweiz), SFr. 205.– (übriges Europa).
    Das Geschenk-Abo mit einer Geschenkkarte wird in meinem Namen versandt.

Preise einschliesslich Versandkosten. Preisänderungen vorbehalten.

- ☐ Ich möchte meine PARKETT-Sammlung vervollständigen und bestelle die folgende(n) noch erhältliche(n) Ausgabe(n) Nr. _______________________________
  _______________________ zu je DM 45,–/SFr. 39.– (bis Nr. 43: DM 35,–/SFr. 30.–), zzgl. Versandkosten (vergriffen: Nr. 1–10, 27, 29–31, 35)

- ☐ Ich bestelle das Werkverzeichnis der PARKETT-Künstlereditionen von 1984–95 (SILENT & VIOLENT, 183 S., davon 144 farbig, Text von Susan Tallman, Kurzbiographien der Künstler) für DM 60,–/Sfr. 49.– zzgl. Versandkosten.

- ☐ Ich bestelle _______ Ex. des Postkarten-Sets mit 36 PARKETT-Künstlereditionen zum Preis von DM 23,–/SFr. 19.– pro Set, zzgl. Versandkosten.

NAME: ________________________________

STRASSE: ________________________________

PLZ/STADT: ________________________________

LAND: ________________________________

TEL.: _____________________ FAX: _____________________

BESCHENKTE(R): ________________________________

STRASSE: ________________________________

PLZ/STADT: ________________________________

LAND: ________________________________

☐ Ich zahle mit Visa ☐ Eurocard/Mastercard ☐ Amex

Karten Nr. [| | | | | | | | | | | | | |] Gültig bis _________

☐ Mein Scheck über SFr./DM _________________________ liegt bei.

DATUM _______________________________

UNTERSCHRIFT _______________________________

Schicken Sie diese Bestellkarte an das PARKETT-Büro in Ihrer Nähe:

PARKETT VERLAG QUELLENSTRASSE 27 CH-8005 ZÜRICH TELEFON +41-1-271 81 40 FAX +41-1-272 43 01

PARKETT VERLAG TANNENWALDALLEE 17 D-61348 BAD HOMBURG FAX 06172-937 444

PARKETT PUBLISHERS 155 AV. OF THE AMERICAS NEW YORK, NY 10013 PHONE (212) 673-2660 FAX (212) 271-0704

FRANCESCO CLEMENTE
GÜNTHER FÖRG
PETER FISCHLI/DAVID WEISS
DAMIEN HIRST
JENNY HOLZER
REBECCA HORN
SIGMAR POLKE
HOLLAND COTTER, BORIS GROYS
MAX WECHSLER, DAVID RIMANELLI
JOAN SIMON, GORDON BURN
GILBERT LASCAULT, WERNER SPIES
BICE CURIGER, JEFF PERRONE
G. ROGER DENSON, VIK MUNIZ
DAVE HICKEY

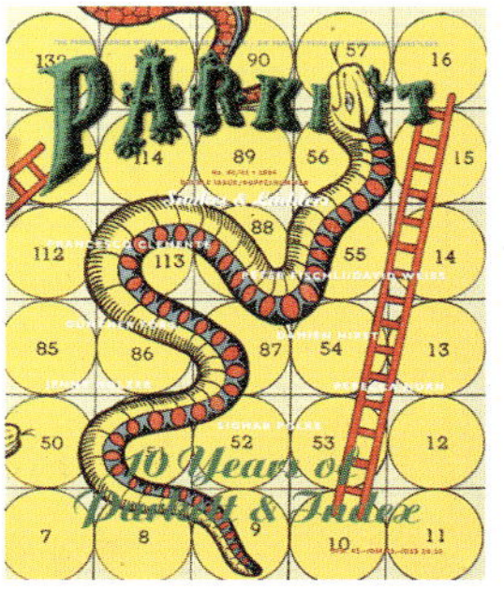

No. 40/41 - ISBN 3-907509-90-0

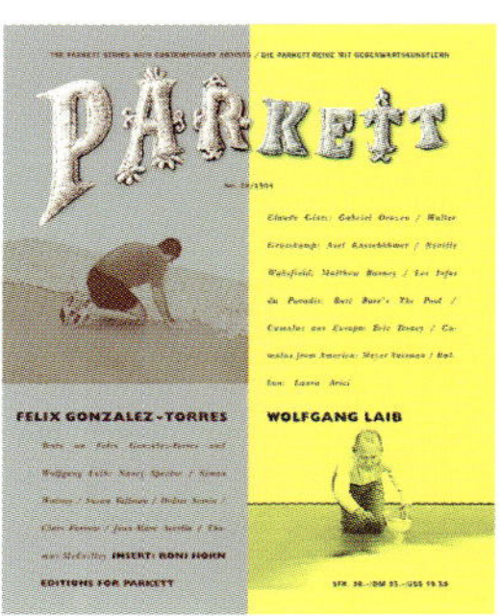

FELIX GONZALEZ-TORRES
WOLFGANG LAIB
NANCY SPECTOR, SIMON WATNEY,
SUSAN TALLMAN, DIDIER SEMIN,
CLARE FARROW, JEAN-MARC AVRILLA,
THOMAS McEVILLEY
CLAUDE GINTZ: **GABRIEL OROZCO**
WALTER GRASSKAMP: **AXEL KASSEBÖHMER**
NEVILLE WAKEFIELD: **MATTHEW BARNEY**
INSERT: **RONI HORN**
LES INFOS DU PARADIS: **BURT BARR**
CUMULUS: **MEYER VAISMAN**

No. 39 - ISBN 3-907509-89-7

ROSS BLECKNER
MARLENE DUMAS
EDMUND WHITE, SIMON WATNEY
JOSE LUIS BREA, MARINA WARNER
ANNA TILROE, INGRID SCHAFFNER
ULRICH LOOCK
INSERT: **RUDI MOLACEK**
HARTMUT BÖHME
MAX WECHSLER: **ADRIAN SCHIESS**
DORIS VON DRATHEN:
RACHEL WHITEREAD

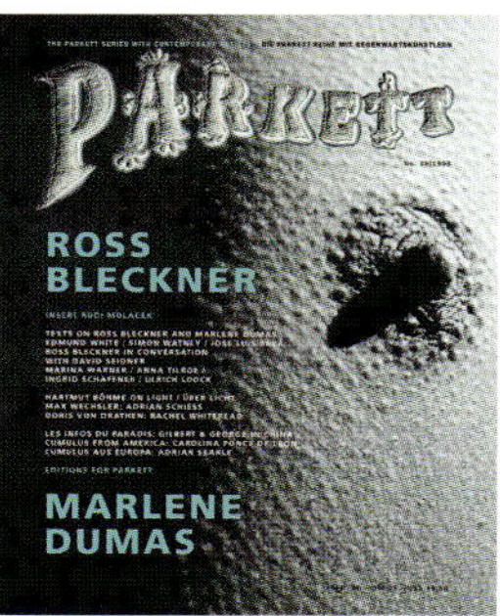

No. 38 - ISBN 3-907509-88-9

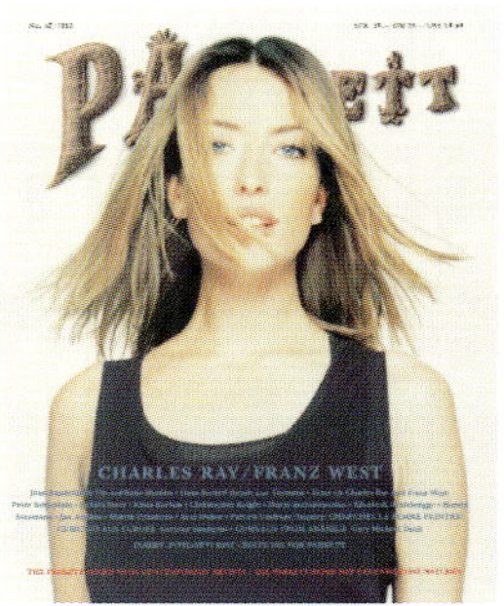

CHARLES RAY
FRANZ WEST
KLAUS KERTESS, CHRISTOPHER KNIGHT
PETER SCHJELDAHL, ROBERT STORR
JAN AVGIKOS, AXEL HUBER
MARTIN PRINZHORN, ELISABETH
SCHLEBRÜGGE, HARALD SZEEMANN,
DENYS ZACHAROPOULOS
INSERT: **PIPILOTTI RIST**
JEAN BAUDRILLARD
HANS RUDOLF REUST: **LUC TUYMANS**
PARKETT INQUIRY:
CHERCHEZ LA FEMME PEINTRE!

No. 37 - ISBN 3-907509-87-0

STEPHAN BALKENHOL
SOPHIE CALLE
NEAL BENEZRA, VIK MUNIZ, MAX KATZ
JEAN-CHRISTOPHE AMMANN
LUC SANTE, JOSEPH GRIGELY
PATRICK FREY, ROBERT BECK
INSERT: **RICHMOND BURTON**
URSULA PANHANS-BÜHLER: **EVA HESSE**
DOUGLAS BLAU: **JON KESSLER**
KIRBY GOOKIN: **LIZ LARNER**
LÁSZLÓ FÖLDÉNYI:
RUDOLF SCHWARZKOGLER

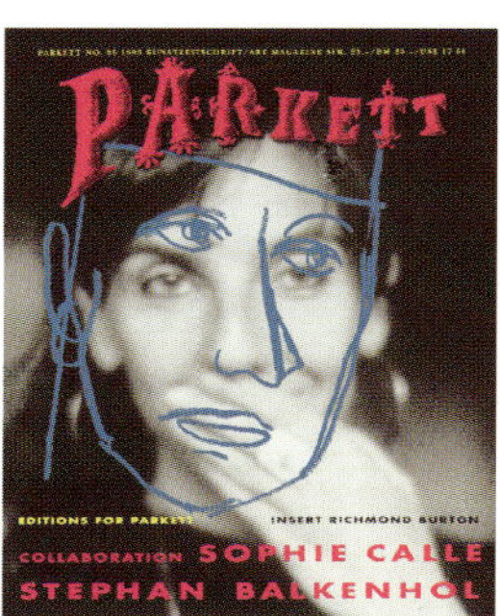

No. 36 - ISBN 3-907509-86-2

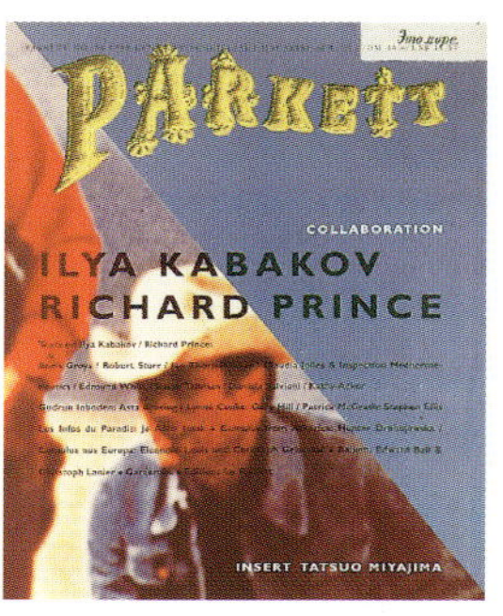

ILYA KABAKOV
RICHARD PRINCE
BORIS GROYS, ROBERT STORR
JAN THORN-PRIKKER
CLAUDIA JOLLES, EDMUND WHITE
SUSAN TALLMAN, DANIELA
SALVIONI, KATHY ACKER
INSERT: **TATSUO MIYAJIMA**
GUDRUN INBODEN: **ASTA GRÖTING**
LYNNE COOKE: **GARY HILL**
PATRICK McGRATH: **STEPHEN ELLIS**

No. 34 - ISBN 3-907509-84-6

ROSEMARIE TROCKEL
CHRISTOPHER WOOL
VERONIQUE BACCHETTA,
BARRETT WATTEN,
ANNE WAGNER, JIM LEWIS,
GREIL MARCUS, JEFF PERRONE,
DIEDRICH DIEDERICHSEN
INSERT: **ADRIAN SCHIESS**
MARINA WARNER: **PENIS PLENTY**
G. ROGER DENSON:
DENNIS OPPENHEIM
CAMIEL VAN WINKEL

PARKETT

WOOL

TROCKEL

33

No. 33 - ISBN 3-907509-83-3

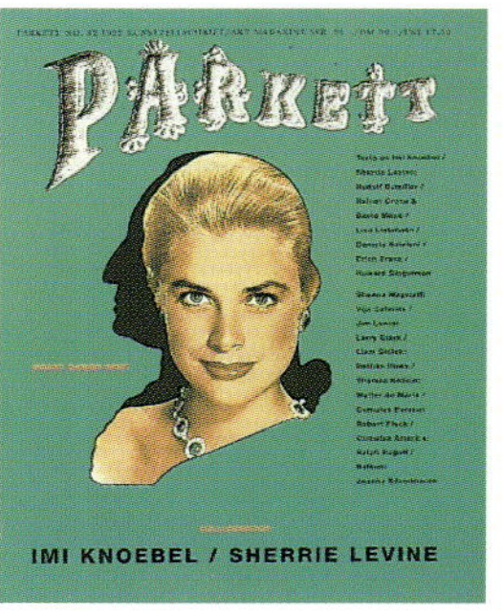

IMI KNOEBEL
SHERRIE LEVINE
RUDOLF BUMILLER
RAINER CRONE/DAVID MOOS
LISA LIEBMANN, DANIELA SALVIONI
ERICH FRANZ, HOWARD SINGERMANN
INSERT: **DAMIEN HIRST**
SHEENA WAGSTAFF: **VIJA CELMINS**
JIM LEWIS: **LARRY CLARK**
LIAM GILLICK: **BETHAN HUWS**
THOMAS KELLEIN: **WALTER DE MARIA**

No. 32 - ISBN 3-907509-82-X